Taking Shape

Elisabeth Rowe

For Celia & John

We looking forward to seeing you over here in due course!

Much love,
Elisabeth
May 2013

Oversteps Books

First published in 2013 by   Oversteps Books Ltd
                                    6 Halwell House
                                    South Pool
                                    Nr Kingsbridge
                                    Devon
                                    TQ7 2RX
                                    UK

www.overstepsbooks.com

Copyright © 2013 Elisabeth Rowe
ISBN 978-1-906856-40-3

All rights reserved. No part of this book may be reproduced, stored in a retrieval system, or transmitted in any form, or by any means, electronic, mechanical, photocopying, recording or otherwise, or translated into any language, without prior written permission from Oversteps Books, except by a reviewer who may quote brief passages in a review.

The right of Elisabeth Rowe to be identified as the author of this work has been asserted by her in accordance with the Copyright, Designs and Patents Act 1988.

Printed in Great Britain by imprint digital, Devon

for Tettan and Alec

Acknowledgements:

Fire Escape was published in Poetry Wales Vol. 45 2009-10
Periodic Tale was published in Poetry on the Lake Journal Two 2009 and Confluence 2010
Growing Things won 1st prize in the RHS poetry competition 2006
Stone Waller and *Stoning the Crow* won 2nd prize in the Virginia Warbey and Wells poetry competitions respectively
kite and flyer won joint 2nd/3rd prize in the Second Light poetry competition 2010
Hoopoes was short-listed in the Stokestown International Poetry competition 2011
Cragfast, *Anything but that* and *Taking Shape* were short-listed in the Wells poetry competition 2012

The following poems were highly commended:
Whale (Poetry on the Lake poetry competition 2012, published in Bestiario)
Last of the Fathers and *Winter Trees* (Torbay poetry competition 2011)
The Bastard (Northampton Literary Group poetry competition 2012)
Fish (Virginia Warbey poetry competition 2010)

Survivor was commended in the Torriano poetry competition 2008 – 9

Contents

Word Turbines	1
Fish	2
Needle Work	3
Toby's Moon	4
Invisible	5
Dolphin Boy	6
Survivor	7
Stoning the Crow	8
Fat Cat	9
Foetal Distress	10
Love Poem	11
Wedding Photo	12
kite and flyer	13
Hedge	14
Yurt	15
Relics	16
Having Learned Nothing	17
Anything but that	18
Our Story	19
The Bastard	20
Falls	21
In the Garden	22
The Burial of the Ashes	23
Growing Things	24
Winter trees	25
Ghost Forest	26
Hoopoes	28
Mountain Flowers	29
Whale	30
Taking Shape	32
Almost Possible	34
Early Morning Tea	35
Fire Escape	36
Cragfast	37
Dartmoor Stone Waller	38
Last of the Fathers	39
Elegy	40

Virtual Life	41
The Body-snatchers	42
Renewal	43
Things	44
Chronicle	45
Memory Lane	46
All Wrong	47
Paint-box Life	48
Work In Progress	49
Periodic Tale	50

Word Turbines

Spin your imagination a little faster
and word turbines like tethered swans
whirling whiter than white wings for the take-off
swing into action.

The shallowest breath will generate
a haiku, limerick or well-pruned lyric;
gusts deliver a sudden epic surge
to the lexicographical grid.

They're all out there, waiting to be harnessed:

>   words from the east to gild the traveller's tale
>   and spice the reporter's story;

>   words from the north frosting the voice of reason
>   for sermonisers, academics, analysts;

>   hot air from the south to fuel spin doctors,
>   romantic novelists and politicians;

>   westerly word-streams veiled in ambiguity,
>   beloved of poets, historians and mystics.

Rhetoric hums like hornets overhead.
Sceptics say it goes to the brain and sizzles
our synapses,
but consider the nuclear option,
fraught with syntactical hazards, nowhere safe
to dump the verbiage.

Give me a word-turbine in my own back yard any day
for clean creative energy, unlimited eco-friendly
renewable word-power
singing along the wires at rock-bottom tariff
to meet my jargon-free targets.

Today words are unavailable:
in conference, or playing multi-dimensional
multi-lingual scrabble.
I stare at the blank page, waiting for my wattage,
wondering if it's time to invest in
subsidised solar scripting.

Fish

The river Lune
too full of itself this spring;
my father islanded on a rock,
the water parting and meeting round him
as he holds out his hand;

and I think it's a rare and splendid thing
to have a father.

But he doesn't see the fish in his shadow
holding still against the flow.

What fish? laughs my brother,
throwing a stone.

My mother says my father goes back to the desert
sometimes, to the tanks, the gunfire,
the puddles they drank from
squirming with parasites –
hard for him to hold still against the flow.

What I see is the arched bridge over the river,
my father's rolled-up trousers,
his feet deathly white on the rock;

my fish, a shadow among shadows,
a visitation,
a point of becoming.

Needle Work

The June day yawns.
Thick bullying heat stills the dance of chalk-motes,
sucks the starch from our gingham frocks,
glues us to our desks.
You watch me through half-closed eyes,
twizzling your chewed red pencil,

and when they file us out into the garden,
settling us cross-legged in a girl-circle
under the monkey-puzzle tree,

your closeness butters my fingers as I clutch
my limp square of cloth
full of holes to poke a bodkin through,
over and under, bossing the stroppy thread
into wobbly rows of cross-stitch.

Too stifling even for sewing.
The monkey-puzzle grates flakes of burning light
onto bare arms,
and when no one is looking, you sneak
a spiked leaf-needle from the dust
and stab soft flesh at my wrist.

One day you will come to a bad end
and I shall try to be sorry,
but this is my first lesson in being hurt
and hurting:

I shall never forget
the blood-beads red as the thread
that slips from the needle's mouth;
never make friends
with any kind of needle work
nor outgrow this queasiness with the world's
sharp appetite for pain.

Toby's Moon

What is the truth of Moon?

Celestial shape-shifter,
once in a blue collusion with
lovers and lunatics;

complicit in night mischief,
wolf-howl, owl-beat,
eclipse of innocence;

silver huntress, gold gondolier,
body-clock, mind-bender,
tide tables turner –

hey diddle diddle,

what is the truth of anything
but waxing and waning,
ebb and flow?

One man's green cheese is another's
'giant step for mankind':
it's all moonshine.

Toby, night-riding his push-chair,
points to his first moon
and cries, 'Sticker!'

Invisible

I'm sitting on a rock that shelters a sandy pool
from the river's rushing, among my children's children,

numbed feet dredging gravelly sand, banking it
high against the water's insidious spoiling.

Downstream the grown-ups are sitting on folding chairs.
They are my children, I am at the edge of their vision.

Their children shoal in the small pool, each pursuing
his own vision of a better world for tadpoles

among tentacles of unnaturally green weed.
The sound of their voices, like wading birds piping,

rises above the noise of the river's rushing.
They do not know they are shoring up the impossible.

I tell them why the banks keep washing away
but not why their own lives will be like that,

water filling their pool and weakening its edges
over and over, while downstream the grown-ups sit

on folding chairs, lulled by the river's rushing.
And with my toes I rake coarse gravelly sand,

making good the walls for my children's children,
almost invisible at the edge of their vision.

Dolphin Boy

Boy in the window seat,
boy with the spiky hair, the orange T-shirt
and eyes of the islands,

silently weeping
behind your Book of Great Adventures and
Britain's Best Jumbo Puzzles,

I watch you take out your carved wooden dolphin
and set it rocking on the table
to the train's cradling;

watch you caress the polished arc of its back,
your wide-set eyes swimming its ocean world,
leaping its beautiful leap,

and I want to tell you
I know what it's like to be leaving
something precious behind.

I want to hold everything still,
stop everything moving forward, moving us
further out of our depth,

and I'm glad when the older boy opposite smiles at you,
and you show him a card trick
and all goes well till the last tunnel

where your eyes become oceans again.
Perhaps someone is waiting on the platform
to hug you and hold your sorrow,

but scanning the sea of faces for my own welcome
I miss whatever brave leap you make
into the future.

Survivor

boys will be boys
will go down to the rocks
daring the ocean
to come and get them

and it will

the innocent waves
the playful dark waves
suddenly heave

seizing the boys
with the fierceness of mothers
the smother of seas

taking the boys by surprise
taking the boys

dragging them down
drowning their salt cries
where greeny-white bubbles
stream upwards to light

one of them lives
the guilty survivor blue as a mussel
flung back to the mothers
like pebble and kelp

the oyster-eyed water ghosts
come in his sleep
come for him now
with their cold webbed fingers

again and again he drowns

Stoning the Crow

They are not looking for harm:

the bird is already injured, flapping
for scrub cover,

a comic hopping dragging thing,
a moving target.

The boys by common instinct bend
to scoop up stones and sling them over-arm,
a gawky war-dance scored with little grunts
and yelps of glee.

The crow shelters beneath its broken wing,
black mess of quill and claw
and splintered beak,

until its eye switches off

and the boys scuff their way to another side-show
a parting kick flecking the soft bird-breast
with crimson.

And in another place someone throws the first stone
a woman spreads her black wings over her head
as the stone splits her cheek
as disbelief reaches her eyes before pain
as she falls to her knees
on the sand

Fat Cat

He was the bad boy who baked his conkers,
peed over the wall into the girls' toilets;
he was the bad mouth who heckled at hustings;
the dream-peddler with the silver forked tongue;
the city slicker with the inside information
and the fast woman in the fast car in the fast lane.
Now he's a fat cat in the corporate playground
where there's no code of practice on bullying,

and I'm shit-scared when I walk into the board-room
and he smiles like a shark with a hearty appetite
till I notice a small scar by his left temple
and I think, I gave him that, behind the bike sheds
one wet Monday, he was messing with my girl,
and I know I'll never get a bigger bonus.

Foetal Distress

It's been a bleak and seamless struggle
from my first uncurling
in this scrawny womb that you pass
like a joint among strangers,

cells screaming to divide,
beleaguered by every kind of stuff
from methadone to mushrooms
and casual starvation.

Slung in my amniotic hammock
I am defenceless against the diffusion
of your rage, your ravenous need,
your soft childishness in sleep.

I have served three consecutive
trimestered sentences and soon
they will finger out the filmy membrane,
cut my umbilical chains:

I shall leave this place trailing clouds
of nicotine, amphetamine, cheap booze,
yet still a messenger bearing the world's
deep longing for lost innocence.

I shall make a space for my separateness,
apprehend things that are now
mere memories of my future,
fainter that foetal heartbeat;

I shall know sound undistorted by
pulsing blood flumes and jacuzzi guts,
colour undimmed by gummed lids;
touch of warm sunshine, pinch of frost.

Yet I am afraid you will not know me
for someone other, that my hunger
will serve only to remind you of your own
and that hurting, you will hurt me still.

Love Poem

You are my poem:
You begin with a-diction
And end with an-alogy.
You have the sassiest ass-onance,
Allite-rate from thumb to thigh –
Search hai- and low-ku
I couldn't meter nicer guy.

And when you s-i-mile at me
You are like no one I ever meta-be-for.
Dare I mention
That you are not a-verse
To my attention,
Even though you may be blank
And I'm for free?

I don't want to be a one-night stanza.
We make a lovely couple-t:
I think therefore I-ambic,
You dac-tyl the cows come home,
And given a bit of rhyme
We might come at the same time.

Don't tell me I'm past my syll-able date,
That you never enjamb-
Meant what you said in bed,
Or that you have a qua-train to catch –
Sonnit! You are my poem, hey!
You have to mean what I say.

Wedding Photo

It might be a game they are playing,
the getting-married game.

They seem to know the rules:

when to exchange chaste kisses;
where to stand framed
in golden stone

smiling at the future.

Yet they know little of each other:
it will be years before they are fluent
in the language of skin;

the crevices, the little cries;

the subtle dance of accommodation
each to other

as age and ultra-violet map
her flawless skin

and the thick flop of his hair
thins and whitens.

Ritual has them by the scruff, for now,
shaking them into submission.

Soon they will hold hands
and sleep-walk down the aisle of years

notching the anniversaries.

kite and flyer

we slip between earth and sky

as light slicks along spider silk
from stalk to stalk

hard to distinguish your being
from mine

sometimes the thread itself
is the more living thing

I feel the wind's tug and snatch
the lift of you away

towards shafts of light
cloud shapes

straining to hold steady against
swerve and plunge

the tremor of your separateness
travelling from hand
to heart

I cannot let you go nor can I
wind you in

kite and flyer
we are playthings of the elements

knowing one day
though we keep it taut between us

the string must break

Hedge

This once-upon-a-time hedge was a row of
well-meant saplings,

with space enough between for looks and love
to pass through.

Was it thuggish time that grew and grew
or everyday neglect?

There was no law of height, no sunlight rights:
the shadows lengthened,

we no longer caught *O sole mio* falling from
our neighbours' bathroom,

no longer sniffed their summer jasmine
rising on the evening air.

Fetch me a ladder, I can just about clamber
slowly, rung by rung,

heart noisy with long-forgotten promises,
right to the very top.

Everything looks neat and tidy: no lawn weeds,
the gravel raked,

a few people strolling around in black suits
and sober dresses,

a small child by the pond, closing his fist
on a dragonfly.

Yurt

The place they enter is a travelling thing,
tethered to such transient sanctuary
as chance provides.

The walls are hung with tapestries and silks,
the air is spiced with their breath;

water falls softly onto stone, and somewhere
a caged bird sings.

They sleep with their hearts touching,
their dreams inter-twined.

They would settle for this,

but the tent must be folded,
its frame dismantled,
bed-rolls bundled and bound,
silks locked away.

They stand bare-headed against
the wind and rain.

Until the next time, they call
as time trundles the yurt on its stony way.

Until the next time.

Relics

she steals his handkerchief
to conjure him from relics
like a shaman

presses it to her face
inhaling pocket secrets
musky otherness

something is transmitted
a direct hit, the shock
of connection

talk to a stone
and it will answer back
but relics prove treacherous

mummify as surely
as slivers of the true cross
bones of ancestors

the body like an ageing clown
performs the same tricks
in a darkened ring

soon the handkerchief enshrines
nothing of him, only
the salt of her tears

Having Learned Nothing

I know this place,

its familiar depth
nudged by contrary tides,
the ghosting of kelp
in a shaft of silver,
sea-bed scurry.

The water is leaden
with guilt, things done
and left undone,
a silt of small harms.

I funnelled my way inside
but the cunning of wickerwork
will foil my exit

until you come for me,
tracking the tiny marker buoy
in vast sea-swell,

hauling me up to light.

How long then
before darkness closes over
and I find myself swimming
back into the trap?

Anything but that

I will not let you go
lightly
away   the distance   west
no more a-roving   awol   on the razzle
to town   to Coventry
to the ends of the earth
the whole hog   the way of all flesh
back   home   against the grain
to bed   to sleep

I will not give you up
easily
for lent   for lost   for auction
for adoption   for grabs
to no good   to a point
above   the chimney   in smoke
for ever

Don't give me up
a gum tree
up the wall   spout   junction   creek
stairs   hill   and away
uptight   side-down   ups-a-daisy
don't give me up and running
to mischief

Don't let me go
off the rails
overboard   adrift   under   missing
mad   bananas   berserk   ballistic
round the bend   downhill   with the flow
for broke   to pieces   to the ant   to the dogs
to the devil   to hell   to perdition
don't let me go gentle
for a song

Our Story

Why not tell our story, he suggested,
when she complained of writer's block.

He sneaked a look at her work in progress,
though he knew it was ill-advised:

she had given him another name
changed the colour of his eyes, and

relocated them from Slough to Budapest,
although she knew he hated goulash.

He couldn't help wondering how she arrived at
so much authentic local knowledge,

and when it came to the sex-scenes he didn't
know whether to be chuffed or disgusted.

He wished she hadn't included his sub-plot
indiscretion with Margot from marketing,

or made the Hungarian psychotherapist
quite so improbably bronzed and louche;

but it was only when he reached the last chapter
that he knew they had come to the end.

The Bastard

An idea came to me in the night,
elegantly poised between playfulness and profundity.

It proved a rough lover
that tied me in knots, tossed me this way and that

until I was satisfied it was flawless,
original and ineradicably mine.

I woke hungry for its embrace
but it might as well have been and gone and never come,

for it had vanished, not the ghost of an idea
to summon back from oblivion –

and I am head-broken, knowing that this
was the ultimate inspirational One True Idea,

and the bastard has found someone else.

Falls

Wind blows, reed bends;
there is no parity,

no law predicting for each love
its equal opposite.

I shall always be salmon to your falls
leaping and leaping

though gravity is on your side

and those who reach the silver spawning grounds
will thrash and thrash.

In the Garden

I am lying
    under the flowering cherry
        making rainbows in my lashes
            the way a child does

when stillness strikes
    a pause in the flow of things
        at the moment of brimming over
            unsolicited

Time rolls over
    like a puppy in sunshine
        things I am paying attention to
            become weightless

I imagine
    I shall always see everything
        through this particular filter
            need nothing more

but as soon as
    the sun begins to spin again
        and wind weaves light in the leaves
            of the snow cherry

grief catches me
    by the throat and shakes me
        I have not loved life enough
            I am not ready

I want to see
    everything one more time
        white lace thrown over blue sky
            the flecks in your eyes

The Burial of the Ashes

We follow the coast-line,
travelling his familiar yellow brick road
through fields of barley, wheat and rye
deep-bronzed with harvesting,
the sea a sheet of blue-flecked silver foil.

One daughter's squeezed in the back seat,
the child on her lap crushing her suitable dress;
the other, next to the driver, nurses the urn,
her tears watering posies still breathing
their garden sweetness.

We tell the old jokes, passing them on.
'Why did the owl 'owl? Why did the lobster blush?'
 (Well, he wouldn't want us to be sad.)
'Why couldn't the viper wipe 'er nose?'

Others are waiting at the cemetery:
the pastor in her holiday frock
reads from Corinthians.
Love is kind, love suffers long, love never fails.
What does anyone really know of love?
Only that there is never enough.

Children peer into the dark hole.
We read their faint familial names engraved
on neighbouring stone: old names, new lives.
The grave-digger with the pony-tail lowers the urn,
tamps down the earth.

Grandpa was a baby once, a child remarks.
Mortality brushes our bowed heads,
flies out over the little red houses
huddled near the sea that is for ever breaking
its journey on rock.

Roadside poppies and chicory
paint the way home as we ask one another,
Why did the chicken cross the road?
All we ever wanted was undying love.

Growing Things

It's one of the oldest stories in the world:
dig and delve, imitate the art of creation,
seek redemption in the grace of growing things,
the innocence of nurture.

Remember how tenderly the old sea-captain
steered his seedling family in their cramped
cabin cots through icebergs calved in the
frozen wastes of Patagonia;

how plant-hunters, dazzled by rhododendron
bleeding on the white slopes of Himalaya,
carried them in the pockets of imagination
to the misty valleys of Cornwall.

Think how one high-rise tenant, hammocking
his petrol can of pansies over the dizzy void,
signals solidarity with all who refuse
to be dispossessed of Eden;

how little children tend miniature moss worlds
in the roots of trees, saucers of mustard and cress,
jam jars with their blotting-paper beans
hopeful on the window sill;

how Irina, prisoner poet, received the gift
of an ice forest ferning the window of her cell,
and knew in her astonishment that one such miracle
may be enough for a lifetime.

Winter trees

Having lost everything they become themselves,

reveal their secret underlying forms,
their true affinity

      with earth and air;

the force that draws them out and upwards

      to embrace the light.

The mathematics of their wayward thrust
is coded in root and branch,

      written on sky;

oak and ash, chestnut, beech and birch
sculpting their own space

      parasol fountain brain

the seeming chaos of their choreography
the work of fractals

      shaping the essence.

In their long sleep trees hold the memory
of green, of softening,

how to coax from wood a gauzy flush of buds

      smoky-rose cinnamon sage

that flare like corals in oceans of blue air,

waiting to unfold
the rapture of their re-invention.

Ghost Forest
Angela Palmer's installation of tree stumps from the rain forests of Ghana, 2009

She strides among fallen giants:
mahogany, denya, dahoma, danta,
a litany of once-upon-a-time leaf-life, lung-life,
no longer cradling cloud, buttressed
against time and rain,
but prostrate like slain goliaths.

She sees how eloquently they could plead for the planet,
exiled from dying forest, laid bare, plinthed
at the feet of the powerful.
And when she's told it can't be done, she wills it
into being, not by magic but by force
of conviction and hard slog.

She oversees the impossible,
their crazy epic journey, the hoist and haul of it,
the long dirt-tracks, the perilous seas.
She clears them for exit and for entry,
cutting a swathe through scepticism,
risk and regulation.

They come to rest:
first in Trafalgar Square, then Copenhagen, Oxford,
majestic testimony to the tracts of rain-forest
erased each second.
What can be imagined can be achieved, she says,
as though trees could teach us
how to save ourselves and our endangered world,
how to move from greed to the greenness
of original Eden.

What lives in the imagination lies
beyond polemic: the solid bone-bare beauty
of dead hyedua, celtis, wawa;

the sliced ringed target of trunk, the shock of root-heart
opened to the light, sculpted and unearthed
from its labyrinthine cast still grasping boulders
in it arms.

These are the roots that anchored the trunk
that worked the fractal wizardry of tree.
Now in the language of the liminal
they conjure ghosts of ancient story, woody mythologies
from latitudes more northerly, of quest and trial
and overcoming, familiar as dreams.

Mahogany, denya, dahoma, danta, hyedua, celtis and wawa are all types of tree found in the rain forests of Ghana.

Hoopoes

It's not only flesh and blood we inherit –
obsessions too may be passed down
like tricks of speech:

the hoopoe was an ornithological icon
for my late parents, and I twitched for
a sight of its motley.

Once I saw a might-have-been hoopoe flash
across a hairpin bend in Tuscany.
It joined the ranks

of might-have-been otters, dolphins and sea eagles,
but at last on a torpid afternoon safari
in the Camargue

when every self-respecting bird should have been
taking a siesta, a pair materialised
as close as you are.

I was scanning the wetland for the White Horses,
those famed poster beasts cantering
through girlish fantasies

all snorting nostrils, flying manes, and hooves
kicking up spray; but two hoopoes
flirting on a fence

were more glorious by far, their black and pink
striped livery, their jaunty crests,
their swooping flight

their simple presence in their proper element
transported me. I was reminded how
in mediaeval bestuaries

the hoopoe returns to care for its ageing parents;
and imagining that fabled paradise
where my father and mother

might be dwelling among creatures beautiful
and rare, I invoked them with a gentle
Hoop hoop hoop.

Mountain Flowers

Someone I knew fell asleep in an alpine meadow
and when he woke to see the silver summit
of Monte Perdido netted in golden lilies
he thought he was in Paradise.

It was enough to send me back to Ordesa,
zig-zagging up to the dizzy canyon parapet
to drown in the perfume of those lilies,
to taste transcendence;

but while I was learning that one man's Paradise
is another's disappointment, I fell in love
with the mountain flowers: not for their lovely forms
or dazzling paintwork

but for the amazing specificity in their choice
of habitat. Botany came in from the cold
as I found myself noticing how each species of gentian
knows its proper altitude;

how a tiny pale cream waxy flower (unidentified)
favours damp mossy places at six thousand feet;
how only on certain slopes of the Alpes Maritimes
will you find white pasque flowers

consorting with riotous red and yellow striped tulips
and sky blue pansies. Flowers are particular:
in a world where order generally makes itself
felt by its absence:

we could learn from them how to know our place,
how to find our own Paradise as peacefully as
Rockwell Kent who died bending down to pick
flowers from the carpet.

Whale

So many false sightings – weed-fin
surfacing from rafts of kelp, wily
water-logged dead-heads –

and still you will not come to bidding,
heaving only a shallow pewter arc
out of grey sea-chop.

This is the long-imagined point
of intersection:
your migratory path and mine;

your biological imperative,
my pilgrimage to celebrate the grace of whale
in ocean element.

One lazy smack of white wing-fin,
one blow of breath-mist is all
your breath-taking bounty,

but it is enough.

Leviathan, they want to make you
more than beast, promote you
to *non-human person*,

declare your right to life, to liberty
and well-being. Look, I welcome
our affinity –

intelligence and self-awareness,
sociable behaviour, language skills –
indeed you may be

more deserving of your rights than we are,
but here and now for me you are simply
whale, heading north,

and I am homing humbled to grey land
where hump-backed mountains breach
snow-silvered from sea-mist,

my gift of life and liberty enhanced
as you dive deep into the heart
of my well-being.

> *Following a meeting of the Helsinki Group in 2010 a Declaration of the Rights of Cetaceans was created. It was discussed at the Vancouver conference of The American Association for the Advancement of Science, Feb 2012.*

Taking Shape

We climb through giant serrated cedars
tall and sacred as cathedrals.
High above no angels, only perhaps
a bleached coffin-boat of bones afloat
on the canopy, wind-whisper of ancestors.

We could believe in transformation here.
Wild creatures of the forest and the deep
hijacked the human story long ago:
eagle and whale, raven, wolf and bear
all unpredictable, shape-shifting on a whim.

Everything may become something else.

We tread the centuries of sponge-soft needles
in reverential silence. Sprawling deadwood
opens strips of light where saplings thrive,
and every tangled root-mass hosts a bustling
ant-encampment.

Everything takes advantage.

Soon we are counting little cairns of scat,
still steamy fresh. The wilderness moves closer.
We whistle jauntily, beat rocks with sticks
and sift conflicting nuggets of advice
on bear encounters: scarper or play dead,
make threatening noises, or (improbably)
establish eye contact, address the creature
in a firm and reasonable manner.

And it is there, and we are unprepared.
Bear, bulked on its hind legs between two trunks:
glint of muzzle, shaggy brownish pelt,
everything about its stance bristling with
superior entitlement.

Stillness. A river talking to itself.
Insects softly gossiping. Our hearts
drumming in syncopated time with fear.
A longish stand-off before bear becomes
stump again.

Everything may be something different:

even we are changed, our laughter edged
with might-have-beens, our trail snaking through
a labyrinth of dark mythologies
towards the falls.

Almost Possible

If nothing is solid, if there is nothing
to separate one thing from another;

if every border is open for crossing
it must be possible (almost possible,

old beliefs being stubborn as trees)
to be at one and the same time

in the place of ice and fire, in earth
and air, this moment and all moments;

and yes, this morning caught between
sunlight streaming and mist dispersing

in a ruined nave of gaunt grey beech
it's almost possible to place one hand

on this world and one on the other
and feel them both solid, beautiful.

Early Morning Tea

For Jo

We are three in the bed
under your mother's narrowed gaze
as she stands squarely beneath the broad blue brim
of her years, within a tilted frame.

Six legs under the quilt
severally aching;
two spoons of sugar stirring my sluggish mind,
still stiff from all that bending and stretching
and stepping in your thought-prints
to reach the high places.

Six feet rubbing together like old friends
while the grey shroud over Blencathra
stubbornly refuses to shift.
Rubbing ideas with you makes fire that will warm the heart
all the long morning and beyond.

I like your face at the end of the bed
cross-hatched with mirth
the way you weave into your story
strands of compassion textured with pain.

We are three in the bed
and most of all I like the way you too face squarely
into the unknown
while the framework of your known world
slips sideways.

Fire Escape
Any person discovering a fire: Sound the Alarm!

    Rain all the way — Wasdale to Borrowdale;
    white streamers flying above the moody tarn.

Emergency Exit Room number 7.
Green sign above the door; white man running
towards white rectangle.

Attack the fire if possible
Using the appliances provided.

    Crouched in the lea of a rampart of black bales
    we mush wet sandwiches, re-lace sodden boots.

I know it's a man — women don't run like that —
but he has no feet. He has used his feet
as appliances for stamping out fire.

    The sun comes out fighting, blazes over Wastwater,
    bloodies the buttresses of Great Gable and Great End.

Moreover he has no hands:
it seems we cannot escape being defined
by the parts of us that are missing.

Leave the building
Close all doors
Report to the assembly point

    Shadow of Yewbarrow creeps up the burning screes,
    encounters night already prowling over Sty Head.

All day my thoughts have been scurrying
in search of an assembly point.

    Framed over the bar Owen Glynn Jones in tweeds
    leans on his ice-axe, surveys unsullied snows.

We sleep rain-fuddled and over-fed
while silently on stumps
white man runs towards white rectangle.

    An owl's flight away clouds of orange vapour
    billow from the cooling towers of Sellafield.

When the Alarm Sounds there is nowhere to run.

Cragfast

A man is spread-eagled on the mountain,
motionless as a gecko, cragfast
beneath a greasy bulge of unforgiving rock
a short pitch from the summit.

Above him a skyful of faces mooning down:
boys bug-eyed with vicarious excitement,
grown men joshing, *Come on, mate,*
you're almost there, only a few feet to go!
They can see his bared teeth, they think he is smiling.

Below him shifting chasms of cloud reveal
green brilliance laid out over tiny fields,
ridges and lilliputian valleys,
neat hedgerows, ribboned roads and
heaven in a lake.

He is stuck somewhere beyond fatigue and fear,
beyond concentration, white knuckles
hooked onto a tiny scrap of granite,
legs splayed awkwardly to meet
invisible footholds.

A baffled raven barks against the cliff,
sound twisted and hurled downwards
by the chivvying wind.
A stone shifts and falls, and falls again.

No one knows quite what to do for this man
who hangs like a child's plaything
suctioned to the window glass, and can move
neither up nor down: there is talk of a rope
and someone takes out a mobile phone
but hasn't reckoned with the mountains.

One by one they hunch their shoulders
in the cooling air and leave him
to the raven and the evening star.

Starlight glitters on his bared teeth
and he is not smiling.

Dartmoor Stone Waller

As a climber's fingertips encode
the memory of each pitch
this man knows stone:

how each has exact and proper place within the whole
not for weight and shape alone
but for the stony self –

its willingness to accommodate,
its habit of resistance.

And stone is plentiful here, tor clitter
for the picking:

he pivots half a ton of granite
with one finger and a crow-bar,

a skill that's handed down,

base boulders first, a double row of giants,
then layer on layer.

He marries the two halves with tie-stones,
fills the space between with Devon earth,
seeded with fox-glove, stitchwort, willow-herb;

slips in his trademark zig-zag seam of river stones,
tops off with copings.

His wall shrugs off water, wind and time;
foot-work of badger, sheep and stoat,
root-work of hazel, blackthorn, holly.

The waller's huge square Devon-red hands
are soon forgotten
but his signature in stone may last
a thousand years.

Last of the Fathers

They keep an artist in their attic, quaint anomaly
for these aged and austere survivors of their Order
now shuffling towards extinction, marooned
in the heart of the city of Westminster. Does the soft
creaking of joints and the swishing of cassock hems
over bees-waxed floors below disturb her dreams?
Are her senses kindled by an up-draught of piety

mingled with sardines and semolina and milky tea?
Easy to see in their simpleness a kind of reproach,
to paint their penance in colours of perversity;
to assume, at the end of their buried-alive lives,
that they are exempt from appetite, immune to doubt
and disappointment, in their bent peregrinations
between cell and refectory, chapel and library.

She listens as they climb with painful slowness
up to the roof garden, where she sits at her easel
more exotic than Eve in a dazzling potted paradise
of surfinias and geraniums, marvelling at the sight
of the bridge that filled Wordsworth's soul with awe,
and the serpent river and the great white face
of Big Ben like an apple she could reach out and pluck.

Here in a waft of jasmine and petrol fumes and prayer
the artist and the old men share their re-creation:
she widens their dulled eyes to once upon a time,
they stir her with the doggedness of their seclusion,
and each sees that the others possess the priceless gift
of looking beyond and beneath the visible surface
and for a moment feels a quickening of the pulse.

Elegy

They told him in November, and he tuned
his spirit to the failing of the year:
bracken bleeding on the hill, the bleached
upland grasses bending to the wind.
When a blustering gale romped down the lane
he watched the starling flock of kids scavenge
in leaf drift, prising conkers from the pallid
moleskin lining of their prickly jackets.

The fungal pungency of autumn woodland
shifted him to a long forgotten schoolroom
where rogue numbers danced inside his eyeballs
as he gazed unseeing at the sleek red pencil
snug in its wooden box with the sliding lid,
and warm urine oozed through his woollen socks.

Virtual Life

And now go into the Sistine Chapel,
point your camera at the ceiling.
Magnifico, that dare-devil master
playing angel on his rickety scaffolding
halfway to heaven centuries ago!

Click! Got it! Summon the others,
study the tiny picture on your screen:
the real thing, luminous, perfect, *piccolo*!
God and all his works in a matchbox
with instantaneous replay.

With your digital eye you are
the voyeur of your own experience.
Click! This is you in a gondola, this is you
in front of the Taj Mahal.
This is you with the penguins,
you and the pyramid, you at Machu Picchu.
And this is you with the baby. Click!

And this and this, innumerable simulacra,
snapped, edited, shared, and stored
to confirm your existence,
fotografio ergo sum,
now and forever.

Don't stop to think you might be missing the point,
failing to see what you should be looking at:
the undiminished essence of the other;
the irreducible beauty of the landscape;
the scale of human creativity;
Adam touched by Divinity.

Keep watching the view-finder, not the view:
be a tourist in your own life,
a hunter-gatherer of images,
a transient in the Sistine Chapel
with eyes only for the infinitesimal replica.

The Body-snatchers

They take me in the garden,
half hidden by a tangle of hibiscus,
hornet-haunted; they capture me
where the shadow of a flag caresses grass
I am requested not to walk on.

They snatch me accidentally
adrift among wedding guests beside the lake,
mesmerised by the perfectly pointillist dance
of light on water.

They snare me in the tropical greenhouse,
my face looming among the improbable
blue-green racemes of the jade vine
like a rare moon.

They snap me in the crypt,
skulking behind the catafalque, a ghost
in the glass casket where San Giulio shrinks
beneath centuries of gilt.

In fragments
I am dispatched to digital limbo,
imprisoned in wallets,
albums, silver frames, unwilling witness
to the world's most far-flung
intimacies.

I should have protected myself,
like Crazy Horse: my soul must struggle
to divide itself into so many parts –
something may have been stolen, defiled,
diminished.

I study the intruders framed
on my own mantelpiece, find no recompense
of life force there: they too are dispossessed,
and I as much the robber as the robbed.

Renewal

We want to be stone,
four-square, commanding,
but we are all glass:
nowhere to hide
from moon's surveillance,
sun's accusation.

When we lift our eyes to the hills
the sky hurls lightning, hailstones,
thunderbolts,
that we shall know our littleness.

The earth casts ordinary marvels
in our path, we reach out,
sensing there is some precious gift
we haven't learned to unwrap.

The hooded moon revives;
leaf breaks from loam;
beneath our feet the bones of the earth
are in shift

but we have had our turn in the light:
*the fruit for which our soul longed
has gone from us.*

Our breath condenses on every cold surface
of the cold world,
the tears of things distilled
in the flask of our years.

Must we still be the comforters
administering salves,
hiding our own sores?

Renewal is the killer,
it wears us out in the end.

Things

The painters are coming:
pale shapes on stripped walls and shelves
mark the absence of things.

Perhaps this is how it should be, towards the end,
a slow severing of connections, a drawing-in;
time to switch off the yo-sushi conveyor belt
of acquisition, to live in a pure white space,
nothing to distract mind's eye.

But these things are my life-combings:
I finger their freight of meaning: the way
this chunk of clear green serpentine polishes the palm of my hand;
how these outsize pine cones from a Tuscan villa conjure the buzzing
of a hundred hornets feasting in the almond tree;
how the little wooden shoe my grandfather gave me houses
a copper sulphate crystal
from my first chemistry lesson.

No one else knows their provenance or can reckon
the compound interest of attachment.
Charity shops are bursting with bric-a-brac
shorn of significance, the leftovers
of our alluvial lives.

Still I am not ready to cast out
my twisted Athabasca driftwood sculpture, silky soft,
my hoopoe tail feather plucked warm from a lawn in Rajasthan,
my mythic sand dollar still leaking silver grains from Mayaro beach:
they are fellow travellers, comrades at the barricades
resisting extinction.

When the painters go
I shall re-instate this treasury, each thing
marking its place in the narrative,
helping me live attentive to the small surprising
marvels of the world.

Chronicle

We tell our stories to be less alone:
yet as I try to chronicle my life
things slip away, the past evaporates.
Forgetfulness like an emboldened scavenger
stalks by day now, raiding the old certainties.

If I were a carpet maker from Kashmir
I would encode my intricate designs
in a written talim, chant it note by note
for the patterning of my plush symmetries
of scroll and leaf and lozenge, knot by knot.

If I were a minstrel of the Mahabharata
I'd memorise a hundred thousand slokas,
envisaging each verse inscribed on a stone.
One by one from the epic heap at my feet
I'd pick the pebbles of my own performance.

But nothing can preserve my ordinary tale,
its currency of words and sighs, the history
of how and where light fell: my spark is dust,
dependent on the sunbeam for its dance,
and each forgetting beckons from the dark.

Memory Lane

I keep asking, has it already started?
The lane is silting with blowsy overgrowth:
I can no longer see the gleam of the road
that ribbons round the hill from the last valley.

Way-marks are revealed in reverse order
dimly as from a half-forgotten dreamscape,
where nothing is ever quite where it ought to be,
deep in the comforting thickets of reminiscence.

Sometimes when I map more recent journeys
I come to a landmark I would rather forget;
Yet I've only to seek a familiar destination
for it to spin clean out of mind's reach.

I keep asking, has it already started,
going the same way again, the same way again?

All Wrong

It was a life of sorts
but somehow it always felt like
the wrong life.

He wrote it in sand
close to the high tide mark:
too much pull of the moon
and all would be erased.

Some of his ideas were novel,
if not arresting,
but critics decided they were
the wrong ideas.

He stalled again and again
on love's sly thermals,
never quite grasping it was
the wrong way to love.

He tired in the end,
like a winter bird that cannot fluff up
enough strength to fly:

he would have known
there were no right words to redeem
the wrong death.

Paint-box Life

Chrome yellow and *yellow ochre*:
I'm trying hard to make it true,
stop the colours running together.
   Look how *vermilion* flowers
   on the pale wash of childhood, how
   sap green, like an acid kiss,
sets the bloodstream fizzing.

Notice patches of deep *cerulean
blue* in the middle distance, a
streak of passionate *rose madder*.
   Now that it's almost finished
   it makes a disappointing picture:
   pains-taking but unoriginal
like painting by numbers, less

than the sum of its parts. I want
to start again, to mix colours
madly, blur my edges, fling
   azure blue and *crimson lake*
   over the *emerald* of my loves,
   oh, and exit with *Titian red*,
blazing like a Viking burial!

Work In Progress

Soon we shall wake up old.
We shall read pity in the eyes of strangers
acknowledging what we have failed to see,
too busy crafting our own narrative to notice
how near we are to The End.

In the beginning
our packs were heavy with expectations –
habits of enquiry, creativity, the care
we owed to the world as the fortunate ones
able to write our own stories,
able to change the plot.

We slew our dragons, accumulated trophies
and mapped the unspoiled landscapes of the mind.
We were happy sometimes, though happiness
like love proved a slippery thing.
We measured ourselves as mothers mark birthday heights
on the kitchen door, calling ourselves to account
for our lack of concern (that old liturgical guilt:
we have left undone those things which we ought to have done)
but like blind bulbs learning to flower again
we hardened after bad winters.

What story shall we tell in the time that is left?
We are work in progress: not till the last page is written,
the last twist of the plot revealed, shall anyone know
what we were, how we added to the sum of things.

It is hard work doing the right thing,
trying to find right words, to pay attention,
not letting age slip its hood over our heads;
hard to exercise laughter, love, intelligence,
mindful of being as well as doing,
learning what is enough.

When we come home to ourselves in the final chapter,
still trying to believe in a better world,
we shall be glad to have lived in interesting times,
glad to let others write the sequel.

Periodic Tale

When I said *Halo-gen!* and he said *Hy-drogen!*
I had in mind a photonic relationship,
nothing physical, just sharing electrons, but he
was so tung-sten and groovy I came out of my shell.

My kid sister said, *Real mole-cule, man;*
my mother asked him to tea-dium: he thought
she was a crashing Bohr, she thought
he was a quark-etypal cad-mium. I said,
I know he's no hel-ium, Mum, and she said,
Iodine, you-odine, please your sulph-ur.

It would have been a quiet wedding, no white stuff,
no phos-phorus, no epithalamium, no tin-tin-abulum,
nothing old, nothing neu-tron, nothing boron, nothing blue,
but came the day he just said, Sorry, I must fly-drogen.
When I asked why-drogen he told me
I was anal retentive, totally upti-gh-tanium,
(To be franc-ium, the sex was only so-sodium,
I regarded with odium all that co-valent bondage
and spin-orbit coupling.)

I said, *Don't be sili-con – you're over-reacting!*
No matter, he was argon-e with the wind
took a car-bon, f-lead by nit-rogen out of my life.
Bye-bye-drogen. Pandemonium.
I fell a-particle. What an a-bismuth failure! I craved lithium.
My mother said, *I told you so – I had his platinum-ber!*
My kid sister said, *Don't get your nickel in a twist!*

I called my brother, laid my soul bar-ium,
said, *Yo, bro-mine, alas-sium-potassium,
the man's done a bunk to Californium!*
He said *Good i-rid-ium! Time for transition.
Get a kryp-ton! That man-ganese-sleaze would have had you
chained to the kitchen zinc and iron-ing y-fronts.
Stone the chro-mium, what an arse-nic-hole!*

Every break-up has a silver lining: by and bi-onic,
I met another guy-drogen – we have affinity!
Plu-tonium ça change. He flu-orine to Gatwick,
gold ring and all. We're in Elysium. What's more,
I have a neon-atal babe, my little ra-dium of sunshine.
(Shhh: don't know the father from Atom.)
Halle-luminum! I quantum-agine a better ending.

Oversteps Books Ltd

Oversteps has previously published books by the following poets: David Grubb, Giles Goodland, Alex Smith, Will Daunt, Patricia Bishop, Christopher Cook, Jan Farquarson, Charles Hadfield, Mandy Pannett, Doris Hulme, James Cole, Helen Kitson, Bill Headdon, Avril Bruton, Marianne Larsen, Anne Lewis-Smith, Mary Maher, Genista Lewes, Miriam Darlington, Anne Born, Glen Phillips, Rebecca Gethin, W H Petty, Melanie Penycate, Andrew Nightingale, Caroline Carver, John Stuart, Ann Segrave, Rose Cook, Jenny Hope, Christopher North, Hilary Elfick, Jennie Osborne, Elisabeth Rowe, Anne Stewart, Oz Hardwick, Angela Stoner, Terry Gifford, Michael Swan, Denise Bennett, Maggie Butt, Anthony Watts, Joan McGavin, Robert Stein, Graham High, Ross Cogan, Ann Kelley, A C Clarke, Diane Tang, Susan Taylor, R V Bailey, Alwyn Marriage, John Daniel, Rebecca Bilkau, Kathleen Kummer, Simon Williams, Jean Atkin and Marie Marshall.

For details of all these books, information about Oversteps and up-to-date news, please look at our website:

www.overstepsbooks.com